I Don't Want to Go to Church!

Turning the Struggle Into a Celebration

Written by
Br. John Mark Falkenhain, O.S.B.

Illustrated by
R.W. Alley

ONE
CARING
PLACE

Abbey Press
St. Meinrad, IN 47577

Text © 2009 Br. John Mark Falkenhain, O.S.B.
Illustrations © St. Meinrad Archabbey
Published by One Caring Place
Abbey Press
St. Meinrad, Indiana 47577

Library of Congress Catalog Number
2009904003

ISBN 978-0-87029-423-5

Printed in the United States of America

A Message to Parents, Teachers, and Other Caring Adults

It is normal and natural for children to go through phases when they don't want to go to church. The reasons and issues involved differ greatly depending on the age of the child. Rebellion by a two-year-old over going to church is certainly different from the resistance of a seven-year-old who finds church boring or difficult to understand. Teenagers sometimes reject going to church for entirely different reasons. In each case, we do best when we avoid power struggles, try to appreciate the child's point of view, and see the resistance as an opportunity to pass on a little bit more about why going to church is important to us.

This book is written for younger, school-age children for whom going to church doesn't always make sense, particularly when it competes with things they'd rather do, like sleeping in or playing. Younger children don't have the cognitive abilities in place yet to understand many of the abstract ideas that go along with faith and religion. For these young people, the experience of church often needs to be more concrete, story-based, or tied to everyday experiences and relationships.

Many churches hold services for children or Sunday school programs for the children to attend while the adults worship. Aside from what happens as part of the service, parents can spark a child's love for church by pairing church time with special family traditions, friendships, or celebrations. In the pages that follow, we specifically mention making traditions out of Sunday breakfasts, coffee with friends, or going to the bakery. Other examples might include picking up Grandma each Sunday for church, or even visiting a friend at the nursing home each Sunday on the way home.

If made fun and enjoyable, little acts of hospitality and charity can make the experience of going to church more concrete, more meaningful, and even something to look forward to rather than resist.

—*Br. John Mark Falkenhain, O.S.B.*

Going to Church

Not everyone goes to church, but lots of people do. Many families go to church every Sunday and sometimes even more often. There are other families who go to church every once in a while, on special occasions or important holidays.

Many families go to church together, but there are some people who go alone. Sometimes that is because they are not married or have no family, so the people at church become a kind of family for them.

In some families, the mother and father go to different churches—usually the churches they went to when they were growing up. When they come home from their churches each Sunday, they might talk about what the priest or minister said. Sometimes in these families, the children grow up going to two different churches.

Why Do We Go to Church?

There are lots of reasons why people go to church. One good reason is that we are all children of God, who invites us to church to help us remember that God made each one of us. If you are not sure why your family goes, you might want to ask your mother or father.

Your mother might say, "We go to church to thank God for all the good things that happen to us each week. Remember the fun we had at the park last Friday? Or how happy we were when Aunt Sue came home from the hospital? These are good things from God; so we need to go out of our way a little to say thank you."

Or your father might say, "We go to church to ask for God's help when we have problems. You know how you are having a hard time at school getting along with Joey? Well, the next time you go to church, you might ask God to help you figure out how to stop fighting with him."

It's a Tradition!

There are even more reasons for going to church. If you asked your grandma why she goes to church, she might say, "Honey, I've *always* gone to church. It's just what our family does on Sunday. I've been going since I was a little girl."

That is what we call *tradition*. Tradition is something that you do over and over again, year after year, for important reasons, even if you can't quite remember them all. Blowing out candles on a birthday cake is a tradition. Putting up a Christmas tree is a tradition, too.

Sometimes we go to church without thinking about all the reasons why we are going. But that doesn't mean it isn't important, or that it doesn't mean anything.

Sometimes I Don't Feel Like Going to Church!

There are times in most people's lives when they don't feel like going to church. Even parents sometimes don't *want* to go, but they *do* because they know it is important.

Getting up and getting dressed for church is not what we always feel like doing on a Sunday morning. You might wish instead to stay in bed and sleep, or watch cartoons, or play video games.

Some children don't want to go because they feel bored in church, or because they have a hard time understanding everything that is going on. Sometimes it is difficult to sit quietly for a long time. Sometimes, though, when we do things we don't feel like doing, we later find out how good or fun they really can be!

Doing Things We Don't Feel Like Doing

Even when we don't *feel* like going to church, it is still important to go. When you think about it, there are lots of things that we do (and *should* do) even when we don't feel like doing them.

School is a good example. What if we skipped school every time we didn't feel like getting up? We certainly wouldn't grow up to be very smart. We wouldn't learn much about math or science or reading or art.

Church is like school because we learn many important things there. We learn about the Bible, who God is, how to pray, and how to make good decisions.

Going to Church Is Like Visiting Someone You Love

When we love someone, we want to spend time with that person, and we want him or her to spend time with us. The same is true with God.

If we want to know and feel closer to God, then we need to spend some time visiting and talking with God. It's sort of like having a best friend or a grandfather. You don't become close to someone unless you spend time together—talking, listening, and learning about each other.

Visiting God's House

God is with us at all times, watching over us, and protecting us. It just makes sense that if we want God to be with us everywhere—even in our home where we live—then we should visit God's house. Church is God's house.

It is special to be a guest in God's house. So, when we go to church, we should try to pay attention to what is being done and said. Don't worry if you don't understand everything. Later, you can ask your parents or Sunday school teacher.

Ask your parents to help you follow along and pray and sing with everyone else. Sometimes everyone will be quiet. When this happens, you can think about how much God loves you. Make up your own prayer, and (to yourself) ask God to bless you and your family and friends!

Seeing People We Know at Church

One of the fun things about going to church is seeing people you know. You might see children who go to school with you or friends from your neighborhood.

If you go to church often enough, you will start to meet new people and you will get to know them. It can be fun to meet the people who are at church with you. Some might even become new friends.

Why Do Some People Never Go to Church?

*J*ust like there are many reasons why people go to church, there are also many reasons why some people choose not to go to church. Some adults have grown up never going to church with their families (it was never their *tradition*!). They don't really know what they are missing.

*O*ther people might think about going to church, or even want to go to church, but have not yet found a church they really like. Do you know anyone who might like your church?

Inviting People to Your Church

A family might wish to go to your church, but might feel shy or worried that they won't know anybody there. They might be waiting to be invited.

It can be a nice thing to invite someone you know to go to your church with you. God loves everyone, and wants everyone to be a special guest. Maybe you can help God make someone feel special like that! If you want to invite someone, ask your parents first.

Church Time Can Be Family Time

Going to church can be a really great time to spend time together as a family.

During the week, we can get really busy. Mothers and fathers have lots of work to do and children have school and homework. There are soccer games, music lessons, mowing the grass, and feeding the cat.

But on church days, everyone can slow down, go to church, and spend time together.

Church time is God's time, but it also can be family time, and a time for all of God's "family" to be together.

Making Church Days Special

Families can do other special things on days they go to church to remind themselves that church days are special days.

For example, you might come home each Sunday morning after church and fix a big breakfast with all of your favorite foods like pancakes or waffles or bacon and eggs. Breakfast is especially good with lots of laughter, talking, and helping out around the kitchen.

While eating, you might try to remember a lesson taught at church or share what you think God is like, and thank God for the fun time you are having together!

Coffee and Doughnuts

Some families might choose to make church days special by inviting friends out for coffee after church. Inviting someone different each Sunday helps to make the people we meet at church feel more and more like friends and family.

If your family loves doughnuts, you might make Sunday special by stopping by the bakery on the way home to let everyone pick their favorite treat!

New Traditions

Special things like big breakfasts, time spent with friends, and trips to the bakery on Sunday mornings can become new traditions for your family.

Traditions help remind us that what we are doing is important and meaningful. Church is a gift from God that brings people together to be thankful for their blessings. So, when we celebrate these traditions with other people on church days, we are sharing God's love for all of us!

Traditions like these might help you look forward to going to church—even on those days when you don't exactly feel like it!

Br. John Mark Falkenhain, O.S.B., is a monk of Saint Meinrad Archabbey and a licensed clinical psychologist. His work at Saint Meinrad includes teaching and consultation in the School of Theology. He also provides psychological services in the local community and does research and writing on the psychological well-being of clergy and religious.

R.W. Alley is the illustrator of all the Elf-help Books published by Abbey Press. He is also an author of children's books. (See a wide variety of his works at: www.rwalley.com.) Alley lives in Barrington, Rhode Island.